THE LORDSHIP OF CHRIST

with chart

Seventh Edition
(Revised)

By the same publisher:

Evangelism
Defective Evangelism
Evangelism Without Apology
Healing for the Mind
The Shepherd and His Sheep
Opened Windows
Heaven's Throne Gift
Invasion of Wales
James Stewart Missionary
Letters from Ruth

© by Global Baptist Gospel Projects Mission, Inc., 1999

Revival Literature
P. O. Box 6068
Asheville, NC 28816

THE LORDSHIP OF CHRIST

by James A. Stewart

REVIVAL LITERATURE
P. O. Box 6068
Asheville, NC 28816

DEDICATED TO

My older Brother David
who was "in Christ before me" and
who, in my early days in Christ,
"expounded unto (me) the way of God
more perfectly."

Printed in the United States of America

PREFACE

HOW SOLEMN are the words of the Lord to Jeremiah and to the people of God: "Thus saith the Lord of hosts, Hearken not unto the words of the prophets that prophesy unto you: they make you vain: they speak a vision of their own heart, and not out of the mouth of the Lord . . . The prophet that hath a dream, let him tell a dream; and he that hath my word, let him speak my word faithfully. . . . And the burden of the Lord shall ye mention no more: for every man's word shall be his burden; *for ye have perverted the words of the living God,* of the Lord of hosts our God." (Jer. 23:16,28,36).

In these strange days the servants of the Lord must be careful to preach the true Gospel. Before the Gospel can be preached clearly, it must be apprehended clearly. The Christian worker must prayerfully and carefully study the great words of the Gospel, and the presentation of that blessed message as found in the Book.

Paul, the greatest of all preachers, exhorts young Timothy, "Study to shew thyself approved unto God, a workman that needeth not to be ashamed, rightly dividing the word of truth." The word "rightly dividing" could be translated "handling aright," or as the modern Greek version says, "teaching accurately" the word of the truth. The Greek word *Orthotomeo,* which is used here, is a metaphorical word. In present-day Greece it is used also in describing a carpenter drawing a straight line to divide a piece of wood. He does not draw a zig-zag line, but straight, and is accurate in his work. He handles the tools aright in following the blueprint, and is thus a workman that needs not to be ashamed.

What is needed, therefore, is not only a mental knowledge of the Scriptures, but a strict adherence to its doctrine, and to the way in which its truths are presented. It was Chrysostom who gave the faithful warning, "He who swerves ever so little from the pure faith, soon proceeds from this to graver errors and becomes entirely corrupted." Only by an assiduous care in the accurate use of the words of Scripture, can we be Gospel workmen that need not be afraid of the coming Bema.

We must firmly hold the blessed evangel, and let neither earth nor hell, men or demons, turn us one hair's breadth from its truth.

Once again, we take this opportunity of thanking our kind friends around the world who continue to spread our messages. We ask prayer for these messages as they appear in magazines in different languages.

May God continue to bless you mightily in your ministry.

Yours in our wonderful Lord,

James A. Stewart

Odense, Denmark   1955

THE LORDSHIP OF CHRIST

CONTENTS

PREFACE 5

SHIFTING THE EMPHASIS 11

THE TRUE MOTIVE 16

THE TRUE EMPHASIS 20

TRUE REPENTANCE..31

THE REBEL'S SURRENDER TO GRACE 36

REFLECTIONS CONCERNING THE CHART........38

ADDENDUM..40

"The evangel bears all the dynamic and dignity of the Throne of God. Its demands cause the sinner to bow in humble submission, worship and reverence before the exalted One Who fills heaven with His glory.

"The paramount theme of the Gospel preacher is therefore the death, resurrection, ascension, and the returning of our Lord Jesus Christ. Also, he must never forget the divine objective to be realized through His redemptive work. This can be nothing less than the proclamation of His Sovereignty in relation to the redemption of men."

REGINALD WALLIS

CHAPTER I

SHIFTING THE EMPHASIS

During the past thirty years we have noticed a gradual, subtle shift in the emphasis of the "Gospel of the glory of Christ," which amounts to a complete perversion of the blessed evangel. The emphasis in our modern day evangelism has shifted from that of the Lordship of Christ to an "easy believism." This shifting of the emphasis has led to an adulterated Gospel and changed the message and the ministry of the Church.

Both movements and men have so often given the impression that the acceptance of the Lordship of Christ is a second experience of grace, or a sort of optional addendum to the Christian life. Peter declared in his apostolic message, "Him hath God exalted with his right hand to be a Prince and a Saviour, for to give repentance to Israel, and forgiveness of sins." (Acts 5:31). *Christian workers today have reversed this Scriptural order and set forth Christ as Saviour first before His office as Prince.* This teaching is nothing less than a complete sell-out to the world, Modernism and Satan. *So great has been the perversion that many congregations are astounded when they hear the true Gospel of the Lordship of Christ.* They believe that we are preaching a new gospel. We know of a certain faithful evangelist

THE LORDSHIP OF CHRIST

who is preaching the same old Gospel which was taught him in his denominational seminary twenty-five years ago. Today that same evangelist, with his message, is rejected by the evangelical churches of that denomination. And for what reason? They accuse him of preaching a new gospel which is but the old Gospel of the Lordship of Christ.

Satan has employed every seductive and deceptive force at his command to cause God's messengers to bypass, or omit altogether, the Lordship of the Redeemer. The reasons for this change of emphasis are not difficult to understand. May we mention some?

First, they want to preach a popular gospel of "easy believism" in order to attract the world to God's message. *They set forth the joy of belonging to Christ, while deliberately omitting the dark background of man's total depravity.* The inference is thus: "That which our fathers taught is old-fashioned. They had a narrow view of the Gospel. It isn't necessary to give up the pleasures of the world and sin. Just believe and be saved."

Second, many honest and sincere Christian workers are so anxious to rescue lost men and women from eternal damnation that they seek to meet the sinner half way. "Yes, it is true." they say, "that Christ is King of kings and Lord of lords, but don't let that upset you. You need not receive Christ as Lord now; just receive Him as Saviour and all will be well." How many times have we been severely pained when some eager evangelist or personal worker has cried out, "Do you believe that? Then you are saved!" Such a parody of truth must not go unchallenged. A sinner can "believe that" and go to hell. A sinner can believe John 3:16 and other Gospel passages and still go to hell.

Third, *in our feverish haste to multiply results by mass production, we lower the standard of the Gospel proclamation.* This is a great day of religious machinery, and the machinery must show huge, immediate results for its propaganda and organization. As never before, the Christian press is panting after sensational news of great results from our evangelistic endeavors. Unlike our Master many workers fail to warn their audiences to count the cost. (Luke 14:25-33). A preacher's success is judged today mainly by the size of the crowds he draws. In John, chapter six, the Saviour preached His crowd away! "Many therefore . . . when they had heard . . . said, This is an hard saying; who can hear it? . . . From that time many . . . went back, and walked no more with him." (John 6:60, 66).

Fourth, as a sop to Modernism we have compromised. There is a definite diabolical master-plan to wed evangelical Christianity to Liberalism. In order to do this there must be a ground of union, and so the doctrine of the Lordship of Christ is thrown overboard. These Modernists deny the fundamentals of the Christian faith. Like the Communists in the use of the word *democracy* these deniers of the Faith have coined evangelical phrases. They have now their own evangelists conducting their own evangelistic campaigns. They will unite with Fundamentalists in union

THE LORDSHIP OF CHRIST

campaigns *with popular evangelists,* but we soon discover that "Their rock is not as our Rock." (Deut. 32:31). It soon becomes evident that what they believe concerning the inspiration of the Scriptures, and the death of Christ, and the contents of the blessed Gospel, is not the same as our evangelical Faith.

On every hand we are told by evangelicals in this God-dishonoring compromise that we must be charitable and not judge the belief of others. "After all, doctrine is not so important: the salvation of souls is the all-important aim." One evil leads to another. When you deny the Lordship of Christ in this compromise, then other evils are allowed in. For example, we know of an outstanding evangelist who declared that although he personally believed in the virgin birth of Christ, it was not an essential belief to salvation. Others are taking part in evangelistic efforts with evangelicals who do not believe in the first five books of Moses as the inspired Word of God. Others do not believe in the atoning, penal death of Christ.

The obvious effect of this unholy wedlock is the lowering of the standard of the experience of regeneration. Another well-known evangelist heatedly insisted that some of the sexiest Hollywood film stars were born-again Christians. What blasphemy! How the angels must weep!

The conclusion to this situation is quite logical. If we can compromise with these Philistines for a month or six weeks in an evangelistic effort, and it is well pleasing to God, then surely we can continue to compromise with them for a life-time. Why not be charitable and invite them to become principals of our seminaries and Bible schools, serve on our foreign mission boards, and preach at our Keswick and holiness conventions?

The desperate need of the hour is for another Charles Haddon Spurgeon to sound the alarm, and raise the banner of God, and fight the foes of the Gospel. The Samsons do not like it revealed that it was Spurgeon's battle with the religious Philistines that broke his heart and sent him to an early grave. It was the failure of evangelical leaders to stand with him in stemming the awful tide of false doctrine in evangelical circles that caused him to pass through great conflicts with Satan which few have experienced.

CHAPTER II

THE TRUE MOTIVE

The grand design of the blessed Gospel is the glorifying of God and the exalting of His beloved Son. When William C. Burns was leaving Scotland for China, a man said to him, "I suppose you are going to convert the Chinese." "No," Mr. Burns replied, "I am going to China to glorify God." Yes, this is the grand design of all Gospel preaching.

We invite the reader to carefully ponder over the following words of A. W. Pink, on their knees before God. They are startling, but true. "If the evangelist fails to make the glory of God his paramount and constant aim, he is certain to go wrong, and all his efforts will be more or less a beating of the air. When he makes an end of any motive to be less than that, he is sure to fall into error, for he no longer gives God His proper place. Once we fix on ends of our own we are ready to adopt means of our own. It was at this very point that evangelism failed two or three generations ago, and from that point it has further and further departed. *Evangelism made the winning of souls its goal, its summum bonum,* and everything else was made to serve and pay tribute to the same. Though the glory of God was not actually denied, yet it was lost sight of, crowded out, made secondary.

"To say nothing here about those cheap-jack evangelists who aim no higher than the rushing of people into making a formal profession of faith in order that the membership of the churches may be swelled, let us consider those who are inspired by a genuine compassion and deep concern for the perishing, who earnestly long and zealously endeavour to deliver souls from the wrath to come; unless they be much on their guard they too will inevitably err. Unless they steadily view conversion from the way God does–the way in which He is to be glorified–they will quickly begin to compromise in the means which they employ. *Bent on attaining a desired object the energy of the flesh has been given free rein; and supposing that the object was right, evangelists have concluded that nothing could be wrong which contributed unto the securing of that end;* and since their efforts appear to be eminently successful, only too many churches silently have acquiesced telling themselves that the end justifies the means. Instead of examining the plans proposed and the methods adopted in the light of Scripture, they tacitly accept them on the ground of expediency. The evangelist is esteemed, not for the soundness of his message, but for the visible results he secures. He is valued, not according to how far his preaching honours God, but according to how many souls are supposedly converted under him.

"Once a man makes the conversion of sinners his primary design and all-consuming end, he is exceedingly apt to adopt a wrong course. Instead of striving to preach the Truth in all its purity he will tone it down in order to make it more palatable to the unregenerate. Impelled by a single force moving in one fixed direction, his object is to make conversion easy, and therefore, favorite passages are dwelt upon incessantly, while others are ignored or pared away.

"In twentieth-century evangelism there has been a woeful ignoring of the solemn truth of the total depravity of man. There has been a complete underrating of the desperate case and condition of the sinner. Very few indeed have faced the unpalatable fact that every man is thoroughly corrupt by nature, that he is completely unaware of his own wretchedness, that he is blind, and helpless, and dead in trespasses and sins. Because such is his case; because his heart is filled with enmity against God, it follows that no man can be saved without the special and immediate intervention of God. According to our view here, so it will be elsewhere; to qualify and modify the truth of man's total depravity will inevitably lead to the diluting of collateral truth. The teaching of Holy Writ on this point is unmistakable. *Man's plight is such that his salvation is impossible unless God puts forth His mighty power.* No stirring of the emotions by anecdotes, no regaling of the senses by music, no oratory of the preacher, no persuasive appeals, are of the slightest avail."

Of course, the Word of God is not bound, nor is the Spirit necessarily circumscribed by the limitation of the message or the messenger. Indeed, such a ministry has often been blessed to the salvation of souls. God, in His sovereign grace, will hear the prayers of His believing people and bless His Word. The light of the Gospel may shine into a darkened soul through a single sentence or through a single verse. We have known the case of a modernistic preacher in the south of Scotland who greatly opposed evangelistic meetings, but who was the means of the conversion of one of his members through the reading of the Scripture lesson from the pulpit!

Neither is it suggested for a moment that every aspect of Gospel truth can be incorporated into one single sermon. Such would be well nigh an impossibility. But it is essential that we do not omit the proclamation of the sovereignty of the risen Lord, which is the dominating principle forming the background of every true, evangelistic appeal.

CHAPTER III

THE TRUE EMPHASIS

What then is the true emphasis in the message of the evangel? The very appellations of the Gospel clearly convey its message; viz. the Lordship of Christ. Here are some of them:

> "THE GOSPEL OF GOD . . . concerning his Son Jesus Christ our Lord . . . declared (designated) to be the Son of God with power. . . by the resurrection from the dead." (Rom. 1:1-4)

> "THE GLORIOUS GOSPEL OF CHRIST." (II Cor. 4:4).

> "THE GOSPEL OF OUR LORD JESUS CHRIST." (II Thess. 1:8).

It is striking to notice that the Lordship of Christ is never divorced from His Saviourhood. Wherever He is presented to us in the pages of the New Testament as our precious Saviour, He is also mentioned as *God's anointed One*.

> "GOD my SAVIOUR." (Luke 1:47).

"A PRINCE and a SAVIOUR." (Acts 5:31).

"GOD our SAVIOUR." (Tit. 1:3)

"The LORD JESUS CHRIST our Saviour." (Tit. 1:4)

"The SAVIOUR, the LORD JESUS CHRIST." (Phil. 3:20).

The angelic declaration sums up the person of our Redeemer: "A SAVIOUR, which is CHRIST THE LORD." (Luke 2:11).

In the New Testament the word *Saviour* occurs twenty-four times, eight of which refer to God the Father as our Saviour. The word *Lord* occurs five hundred and twenty-two times; *Lord Jesus* thirty times; and the *Lord Jesus Christ* eighty-one times. In the book of The Acts our precious Redeemer is called *Saviour* only twice– "Him hath God exalted. . . to be a Prince and a Saviour." (Acts 5:31); and, "Of this man's seed hath God according to his promise raised unto Israel a Saviour." (Acts 13:23). On the other hand it is amazing to notice that the title "Lord" is mentioned ninety-two times; "Lord Jesus" thirteen times; and the "Lord Jesus Christ" six times, in the same book.

Throughout the Acts of the Apostles we find that *Jesus is presented as the risen, glorified Christ* at the Father's right hand. "This Jesus hath God raised up, whereof we all are witnesses. Therefore being by the right hand of God exalted, and having received of the Father the promise of the Holy Ghost, he hath shed forth this, which ye now see and hear. For David is not ascended into the heavens: but he saith himself, The Lord said unto my Lord, Sit thou on my right hand, Until I make thy foes thy footstool. Therefore let all the house of Israel know assuredly, that *God hath made that same Jesus, whom ye have crucified, both Lord and Christ."* (Acts 2:32-36). Nowhere do we have such an insight into the contents of the Gospel message as in the apostolic sermons in this book. Here we see the titles of our blessed Redeemer used with the Spirit's guidance and discretion. Here is the Gospel clear and plain. As we study carefully, sentence by sentence, we discover that *they preached Jesus Christ as Lord.* "For we preach not ourselves, but Christ Jesus the Lord; and ourselves your servants for Jesus' sake." (II Cor. 4:5).

We note that the emphasis is not so much on the death of Christ as on His resurrection; not so much on His Saviourhood as on His Lordship. The Apostles' was a three-fold message: The resurrection, the ascension, and consequently, the Lordship of Christ. Although it is true that Christ said, "Therefore doth my Father love me, because I lay down my life, that I might take it again. No man taketh it from me, but I lay it down of myself. I have power to lay it down, and I have power to take it again" (John 10:17-18)! Nevertheless, *the early evangelists stressed that it was God the Father Who raised His beloved Son from the tomb.*

THE LORDSHIP OF CHRIST

"Whom God hath raised up" (Acts. 2:24).

"This Jesus hath God raised up" (Acts 2:32).

"Whom God hath raised from the dead" (Acts 3:15).

"God, having raised up his Son Jesus" (Acts 3:26).

"Jesus Christ of Nazareth . . . whom God raised from the dead" (Acts 4:10).

"The God of our fathers raised up Jesus" (Acts 5:30).

"Him God raised up the third day" (Acts 10:40).

"[God] . . . raised him from the dead" (Acts 17:31).

Romans chapter ten and verse nine is a Gospel classic for the unsaved. We discover here that if you confess with your lips that Jesus is Lord and believe in your heart that God raised him from the dead, you will be saved. We see in this verse two things which are essential for salvation—confession with the mouth and belief in the heart. The heart is the symbol of the inner life, while the mouth is the symbol of the outer life. "Out of the abundance of the heart the mouth speaketh" (Matt. 12:34). *There must be a heart belief in the resurrection of the Lord Jesus.* To believe that God raised Him from the dead, is to believe in the finality and efficacy of His

THE LORDSHIP OF CHRIST

atoning sacrifice. To believe in the resurrection of Christ, is to believe that the precious blood of the Lamb silenced the thunderings of Mount Sinai. To believe that God raised His Son from the dead, is to believe that Christ met the righteous claims of a holy God against the repentant sinner. God stamped His divine approval upon the sacrificial work of His Son in that He raised Him from the dead on the third day. This is the glorious news of the Gospel of the risen Redeemer!

> Guilty, vile and helpless we,
> > Spotless, Lamb of God was He;
> "Full atonement!" can it be?
> > Hallelujah! What a Saviour!
> Lifted up was He to die,
> > "It is finished," was His cry:
> Now is Heaven exalted high,
> > Hallelujah! What a Saviour!

The death of Christ was the payment for our sins, and the resurrection was the receipt. "Who was delivered for our offences, and was raised again for our justification" (Rom. 4:25).

There must be a confession of Jesus as Lord of the life. Although this includes a public confession of our faith in Christ as Redeemer, it is plainly evident from the New Testament that it also involves the acknowledgement of the entire life to live under the Lordship of Christ. That this confession is not a mere lip

THE LORDSHIP OF CHRIST

service is clearly evident from the words of the Saviour, "Not every one that saith unto me, Lord, Lord, shall enter into the kingdom of heaven; but he that doeth the will of my Father which is in heaven" (Matt. 7:21). Paul warns the Corinthian believers, "No man can say that Jesus is the Lord, but by the Holy Ghost" (I Cor. 12:3). Only by the miracle of regeneration and a transformed life is a man able to call Jesus the Lord.

We next discover in the apostolic evangel the preaching of an ascended Lord to the Father's right hand in power and glory.

> "Therefore being by the right hand of God exalted" (Acts 2:33).
>
> "The God of Abraham, and of Isaac, and of Jacob, the God of our fathers, hath glorified his Son Jesus" (Acts 3:13).
>
> "This is the stone which was set at nought of you builders, which is become the head of the corner" (Acts 4:11).
>
> "Behold, I see the heavens opened, and the Son of Man standing on the right hand of God" (Acts 7:56).

The triumphant entry of our glorious Redeemer into the courts of Heaven is tersely expressed by the Holy Ghost in the words, "Received up into glory" (I Tim. 3:16).

THE LORDSHIP OF CHRIST

The Scripture affords the clearest proof of the triumphant manner in which the Lord of life and glory went up on high. In Psalm 68 there is a blessed description of the glorious convoy of angels which attended Him on His royal progress up to Heaven's gates. For even as when He will appear the second time without sin unto salvation, He will be "revealed from heaven with his mighty angels" (II Thess. 1:7 and Matt. 16:27), so also did thousands upon thousands of ministering angels attend upon Him at His triumphant ascension. "The chariots of God are twenty thousand, even thousands of angels: the Lord is among them, as in Sinai, in the holy place. Thou hast ascended on high, thou hast led captivity captive: thou hast received gifts for men; yea, for the rebellious also, that the Lord God might dwell among them" (Psa. 68:17-18).

This triumphant ascension of the blessed Lord is also clearly intimated in Psalm 47: "O clap your hands, all ye people; shout unto God with the voice of triumph. For the Lord most high is terrible; he is a great King over all the earth . . . God is gone up with a shout, the Lord with the sound of a trumpet. Sing praises to God, sing praises: sing praises unto our King, sing praises. For God is the King of all the earth: sing ye praises with understanding" (Psa. 47:1-2, 5-7).

Nor are we left without scriptural intimations even of *the blessed Lord's reception in the courts of glory.* When He reached the gates of Heaven the celestial courts were, as it were, moved at His approach, for then was accomplished that memorable transition recorded in

Psalm 24 as thus represented to our faith. It was as if the attendant angels that formed His glorious convoy shouted aloud before Him as the heralds of His approach, "Lift up your heads, O ye gates; and be ye lift up, ye everlasting doors; and the King of glory shall come in" (Psa. 24:7). But from within is made the inquiry, "Who is this King of glory?" The answer is given from without by the attendants of His train of triumph, "The Lord strong and mighty, the Lord mighty in battle." Then comes forth the universal chorus from without and from within, "Lift up your heads, O ye gates; even lift them up, ye everlasting doors; and the King of glory shall come in. Who is this King of glory? The Lord of hosts, he is the King of glory" (Psa. 24:9,10).

In another scripture the Lord is represented in His glorious ascension as the conquering Christ dragging at His chariot wheels the infernal hosts of hell and openly showing them to all the holy angels as vanquished prisoners. "And you, being dead in your sins and the uncircumcision of your flesh, hath he quickened together with him, having forgiven you all trespasses; Blotting out the handwriting of ordinances that was against us, which was contrary to us, and took it out of the way, nailing it to his cross; And having spoiled principalities and powers, he made a shew of them openly, triumphing over them in it" (Col. 2:13-15).

> Look, ye saints, the sight is glorious,
> See the "Man of Sorrows" now;

> From the fight return victorious,
> > Every knee to Him shall bow.
> Crown Him, crown Him!
> > Crowns become the Victor's brow,
>
> Crown the Saviour! Angels crown Him!
> > Rich the trophies Jesus brings;
> In the seat of power enthrone Him,
> > While the vault of Heaven rings,
> Crown Him! crown Him!
> > Crown the Saviour King of Kings.

What a glorious truth is that of the ascension of our blessed Lord. It was Peter's explanation of the phenomeon of Pentecost (Acts 2:33). Why are there so few hymns on the ascension of Christ?

Since His ascension His official title is, "The Lord Jesus Christ." "God hath made that same Jesus, whom ye have crucified, both Lord and Christ" (Acts 2:36). This is the official royal proclamation from heaven. "Him hath God exalted . . . to be a Prince and a Saviour" (Acts 5:31). The name *Jesus* occurs six hundred and eight times before the ascension, and only sixty-two times afterwards.* It is used thirty times in the Acts alone, which is about half the number, to prove that Jesus of Nazareth is now the Enthroned One and Conqueror. The name *Jesus,* by itself, is mentioned in the Epistles thirty-two times, and like the references in the Acts is used with deep significance to prove the

---

* *See Chart*

Lordship of Christ. Two passages will suffice to illustrate this fact:

"Wherefore God also hath highly exalted him, and given him a name which is above every name: That at the name of Jesus every knee should bow, of things in heaven, and things in earth, and things under the earth; And that every tongue should confess that JESUS CHRIST IS LORD, to the glory of God the Father" (Phil. 2:9-11); and, "Whosoever believeth that Jesus *is the Christ* is born of God" (I John 5:1).

It is striking to notice that the title of "The Lord Jesus Christ" never appears before the ascension, and that it occurs some eighty-one times afterwards. There is a tendency today to declare the Saviour's death on the Cross for sinners and that alone! While the essential basis of the true Gospel appeal must ever be "Christ crucified," it must never leave the hearers with a crucified Christ. *The plain fact is that Christ on the Cross can save nobody.* The atoning sacrifice of Calvary and the shedding of His precious blood is the foundation of our salvation. But it is a RISEN LORD and that alone which saves. The New Testament Gospel message includes, by presupposition, that Calvary opened up a way whereby a holy God could justify a hell-deserving sinner. "Being justified freely by his grace through the redemption that is in Christ Jesus" (Rom. 3:24).

It must not be overlooked that when Jesus is received as Lord, He must be received as a crucified Lord. The One Who is now exalted "in the midst of the throne" is represented as a "Lamb as it had been slain" (Rev. 5:6). It is not as though He was Christ only in His sufferings for us, and is now Lord since His exaltation. No, He was "the Lord of glory" when He was crucified; and it is as the "Lamb that was slain" that He now receives the worship of the redeemed in Heaven (Rev. 5:11,12). So then it is as the crucified Lord that He must reign in our hearts now. To receive the crucified One as our Lord means to be despised and rejected with Him. We must bear the stigma and the reproach of the Cross of Christ. *The acceptance of Christ as Lord means also the crucifixion of the old life of selfishness and sin.* "They that are Christ's have crucified the flesh with the affections and lusts" (Gal. 5:24). If the crucified One is Lord of our lives, the hand that rules will be a nail-pierced hand. He, as the Captain of our Salvation, will lead us in a path of crucifixion and shame. That is what it means to accept Christ as Lord.

CHAPTER IV

TRUE REPENTANCE

There are many who want to be saved from the consequences of their sin, who do not want to be saved from the love of it. *Many want to be delivered from sin's curse and sin's wages, who do not want to bow their neck to the yoke of Christ.* There are many who are attracted by the Gospel message and see the way of salvation, who are still possessing a craving for this present evil age. How great the need for care, lest by an inadequate presentation of the truth of the Gospel we deceive these souls into a false profession. There is a grave danger that many people will make a mistake of substituting an emotional religious crisis for a born-again experience. To preach Christ as Saviour without preaching Christ as Lord, makes a mockery of the Gospel and the entire Christian life. There must be true repentance. "If any man love the world, the love of the Father is not in him" (I John 2:15).

To those who want to receive Christ as Saviour in order to have a passport to Heaven, but desire to remain in their sins and in the world, we must be faithful and declare like Peter, "Thou hast neither part nor lot in this matter: for thy heart is not right in the sight of God. Repent therefore of this thy wickedness, and pray God, if perhaps the thought of thine heart may be forgiven thee. For I perceive that thou art in the gall of bitterness, and in the bond of iniquity" (Acts 8:21-23).

Mr. Spurgeon warns his students: "If the professed convert distinctly and deliberately declares that he knows the Lord's will but does not mean to attend to it, you are not to pamper his presumption, but it is your duty to assure him that he is not saved. Do you imagine that the Gospel is magnified or God glorified by going to the worldlings and telling them that they may be saved at this moment by simply accepting Christ as their Saviour, while they are wedded to their idols and their hearts are still in love with sin? If I do so, I tell them a lie, pervert the Gospel, insult Christ, and turn the grace of God into lasciviousness."

The Son of God does not save rebels. There must be true submission (repentance) before there can be salvation. What a parody of the Gospel when many are told to "trust Jesus to take them to Heaven when they die," who nevertheless are living in the practice of sin and rebellion against His laws.

Mr. George Goodman has left on record an illustration of the truth of the utter hollowness or utter impossibility of claiming to rest on "the finished work of Christ," while refusing to live under the Lordship of Christ: "A king has part of his kingdom in rebellion, and in order to show his grace, causes mercy to be proclaimed to the rebels on their yielding to him and seeking reconciliation on the ground of the proclamation. He threatens destruction to those who continue to defy his authority. One of the rebels is warned of his danger, but he replies, 'I am in no danger; I am resting on the proclamation; I am sure the king is faithful. He will never break his promise or withdraw his proclaimed mercy.'

"'But you are still in rebellion. You are continuing in the course he condemns, and are indifferent to His commands, and the mercy is offered to those who yield.'

"'True, but the mercy is free; there are no conditions, and to make conditions would be to make it no more of grace,' is the reply.

"What should we say to such reasoning? Alas, is it not in effect what some of us say who, while refusing Christ as Lord, profess to trust in Him and His work for salvation?"

Walter Marshall wrote some three hundred years ago, "Why doth a man seek a pardon if he intends to go on in rebellion and stand out in defiance of his prince? They seek a pardon in a mocking way and intend not to return unto obedience . . . To take a part of His salvation and leave out the rest? But Christ is not divided . . . They would be saved by Christ and yet be out of Christ in a fleshly state, whereas God doth free none from condemnation, but those who are IN Christ."

"There is forgiveness with thee, that thou mayest be feared" (Psa. 130:4). Many of God's children forget, when dealing with the unsaved, that *the grace of God does not give deliverance to the sinner from the penalty of his sins and then give him liberty to live a life of sin.* Paul tells us that the pardoning grace of God teaches us

THE LORDSHIP OF CHRIST

to live a life of holiness: "Teaching us that, denying ungodliness and worldly lusts, we should live soberly, righteously, and godly, in this present world; Looking for that blessed hope, and the glorious appearing of the great God and our Saviour Jesus Christ; Who gave himself for us, that he might redeem us from all iniquity, and purify unto himself a peculiar people, zealous of good works. These things speak, and exhort, and rebuke with all authority. Let no man despise thee" (Tit. 2:12-15).

The teaching is clear in the Epistles that if a person has passed from death unto life he is now under the sway of the Lordship of Christ. "For the love of Christ constraineth us; because we thus judge, that if one died for all, then were all dead: And that he died for all, that they which live should not henceforth live unto themselves, but unto him which died for them, and rose again . . . Therefore if any man be in Christ, he is a new creature: old things are passed away; behold, all things are become new" (II Cor. 5:14-17). The young convert is now UNDER NEW MANAGEMENT.

Paul's conversion is the pattern conversion of the New Testament. His first words in his new life in Christ were, "Lord, what wilt thou have me to do?" Yes, the first word of a new-born soul is *Lord*. The Lord takes control of the heart that receives Him as Saviour and makes known His will. The believer knows His voice and rejoices to obey. "My sheep hear my voice, and I know them, and they follow me" (John 10:27).

Let me finish with an incident in my evangelistic experience. When I was preaching in the open air in Scotland, I invited the listening crowd to come forward and accept the Gospel of John in my hand if they were interested or anxious to be saved. Immediately a young girl of fourteen years of age came forward and received a copy. "Why do you want to be saved?" I asked. "Why do you want to accept Christ as your Saviour?" The answer came clear as crystal, "Please sir, I do not want to live a life of sin." John D. Wheeler, my colleague (an aged, experienced worker, having laboured with Dr. Torrey and Gypsy Smith) said that this was the finest answer ever given to this all-important question.

Oh, my fellow Christian workers, let us cease proclaiming a perverted Gospel, and preach the evangel of COMPLETE SALVATION: Jesus Christ Lord. "The grace of our Lord Jesus Christ be with you all. Amen."

THE REBEL'S SURRENDER TO GRACE

"Lord, what wilt Thou have me to do?" (Acts 9:6).

Lord, thou hast won, at length I yield;
My heart, by mighty grace compell'd
    Surrenders all to thee:
Against thy terrors long I strove,
But who can stand against Thy love?
    Love conquers even me.

All that a wretch could do, I try'd,
Thy patience scorn'd, thy pow'r defy'd,
    And trampled on thy laws;
Scarcely thy martyrs at the stake
Could stand more steadfast for thy sake,
    Than I in Satan's cause.

But since thou hast thy love reveal'd,
And shown my soul a pardon seal'd,
    I can resist no more:
Couldst thou for such a sinner bleed?
Canst thou for such a rebel plead?
    I wonder and adore!

If thou hadst bid thy thunders roll,
And lightnings flash, to blast my soul,

I still had stubborn been;
But mercy has my heart subdu'd,
A bleeding Saviour I have view'd,
   And now I hate my sin.

Now, Lord, I would be thine alone,
Come, take possession of thine own,
   For thou hast set me free;
Releas'd from Satan's hard command,
See all my powers waiting stand,
   To be employe'd by thee.

My will, conform'd to thine, would move;
On thee, my hope, desire, and love,
   In fix'd attention join:
My hands, my eyes, my ears, my tongue,
Have Satan's servants been so long,
   But now they shall be thine!

And can I be the very same
Who lately durst blaspheme thy name,
   And on thy gospel tread?
Surely each one who hears my case,
Will praise thee, and confess thy grace
   Invincible indeed!

John Newton
(Author of *Amazing Grace*)

REFLECTIONS CONCERNING THE CHART

In order that the reader may see for himself the significance of the titles of the Lord, we have prepared the following table, with the fifteen names, titles, and combinations used concerning our Lord Jesus Christ.

The thing that strikes us at a glance is that the simple earthly name of "Jesus" is quoted profusely before the ascension and rarely after the ascension. For example, the name "Jesus" occurs 608 times before the ascension, and only 62 times after. It is used 30 times alone in the Acts of the Apostles, thus taking up half the number, to prove that Jesus of Nazareth was the promised Messiah.

"Jesus of Nazareth . . . ye have taken, and by wicked hands have crucified and slain . . . Whom God hath raised up." (Acts 2:22-24).

"Jesus hath God raised up" (Acts 2:32).

"The God of Abraham . . . hath glorified His Son Jesus" (Acts 3:13).

The name "Jesus" by itself in the Epistles scarcely exceeds a score, and like those in the Acts of the Apostles, used with deep significance, to prove His Lordship. The classic passage of Philippians, second chapter, will suffice: "Who, being in the form of God, thought it not robbery to be equal with God: But made himself of no reputation, and took upon him the form of a servant, and was made in the likeness of men: And being found in fashion as a man, he humbled himself, and became obedient unto death, even the death of the cross. Wherefore God also hath highly exalted him, and given him a name which is above every name. That at the *name of Jesus* every knee should bow, of things in heaven, and things in earth, and things under the earth; And that every tongue should confess that *Jesus Christ is Lord,* to the glory of God the Father (v. 6-11)."

As we continue to glance at the chart, we notice that the name "Jesus" occurs only fourteen times in Paul's epistles. It occurs eight times in the Epistle to the Hebrews, where the writer is stressing the sufferings of the humanity of Christ as our great High Priest.

In Galatians, Colossians, II Thessalonians, I and II Timothy, Titus, Philemon, James, I and II Peter, II and III John, and Jude, the name "Jesus" never appears alone.

You will notice again that the title "The Lord Jesus Christ" is never mentioned before the ascension, and that it occurs eighty-one times after. "Christ Jesus our Lord" occurs seven times; "Christ Jesus the Lord," twice.

The entire revelation of the Word of God closes with His majestic title: "The grace of our *Lord Jesus Christ* be with you all. Amen."

ADDENDUM

"Jesus Christ" describes the Incarnate One, Who through His death purchased redemption for us, and is now the living and glorified Redeemer.

"Christ Jesus" describes the eternal Son, Who humbled Himself, even to the shameful death of the Cross.

"Jesus Christ" suggests His glory; "Christ Jesus" suggests His grace.

The title "Christ" suggests a relation of Jesus to God rather than to man. It would be wrong to refer to Him as "Our Christ." He is always and only God's Christ.

> "And it was revealed unto him by the Holy Ghost, that he should not see death, before he had seen the Lord's Christ" (Luke 2:26).

> "He said unto them, But whom say ye that I am? Peter answering said, The Christ of God" (Luke 9:20).

> "And the people stood beholding. And the rulers also with them derided him, saying, He saved others; let him save himself, if he be Christ, the chosen of God [If He be the Christ of God]" (Luke 23:35).

"The kings of the earth stood up, and the rulers were gathered together against the Lord, and against his Christ" (Acts 4:26).

"The kingdoms of this world are become the kingdoms of our Lord, and of his Christ" (Rev. 11:15).

"Now is come salvation, and strength, and the kingdom of our God, and the power of his Christ" (Rev. 12:10).

"And ye are Christ's; and Christ is God's (I Cor. 3:23).

The reason that the Redeemer is God's Christ is obvious. The title "Christ" is equivalent to the Hebrew word "Messiah" and signifies the anointed. Jesus is God's anointed, and not man's.

See Chart
Next Page

BOOK	JESUS	CHRIST	LORD	JESUS CHRIST	CHRIST JESUS	LORD JESUS	LORD CHRIST	JESUS OUR LORD	CHRIST THE LORD	LORD JESUS CHRIST	CHRIST JESUS OUR LORD	CHRIST JESUS THE LORD	JESUS CHRIST OUR LORD	CHRIST JESUS MY LORD	JESUS CHRIST LORD & SAVIOUR
BEFORE ASCENSION															
Matthew	170	13	51	2	—	—	—	—	—	—	—	—	—	—	—
Mark	94	6	17	1	—	—	—	—	—	—	—	—	—	—	—
Luke	98	12	85	—	—	1	—	—	1	—	—	—	—	—	—
John	246	19	43	2	—	—	—	—	—	—	—	—	—	—	—
AFTER ASCENSION															
Acts	30	14	92	10	1	13	—	—	—	6	—	—	—	—	—
Romans	2	35	26	13	6	2	—	1	—	9	—	—	5	—	—
I Cor.	2	47	53	6	3	3	—	—	—	10	—	—	1	—	—
II Cor.	5	38	21	6	—	3	—	—	—	4	—	1	—	—	—
Gal.	—	24	2	8	5	1	—	—	—	3	—	—	—	—	—
Eph.	1	27	17	5	6	1	—	—	—	7	1	—	—	—	—
Phil.	1	18	10	9	8	1	—	—	—	2	—	—	—	1	—
Col.	—	19	8	1	2	1	1	—	—	2	—	1	—	—	—

I Thess. ..	3	3	13	—	2	2	—	—	—	9	—	—	—	—	—
II Thess. ..	—	2	10	—	—	1	—	—	—	9	—	—	—	—	—
I Tim. ..	—	2	3	3	5	—	—	—	—	4	—	1	—	1	—
II Tim. ..	—	1	14	3	7	—	—	—	—	2	—	1	—	—	—
Titus ..	—	—	—	3	—	—	—	—	—	1	—	—	—	—	—
Philemon	—	1	3	2	2	—	—	—	—	2	—	—	—	—	—
Hebrews ..	8	9	16	3	1	1	—	—	—	—	—	—	—	—	—
James ..	—	—	12	—	—	—	—	—	—	2	—	—	—	—	—
I Peter ..	—	10	5	9	2	—	—	—	1	1	—	—	—	—	—
II Peter ..	—	—	10	2	—	—	—	—	—	3	—	—	—	—	3
I John ..	4	2	—	8	—	—	—	—	—	—	—	—	—	—	—
II John ..	—	2	—	1	—	—	—	—	—	1	—	—	—	—	—
III John ..	—	—	—	—	—	—	—	—	—	—	—	—	—	—	—
Jude ..	—	—	3	2	—	—	—	—	—	3	—	—	—	—	—
Rev. ..	6	4	8	6	—	—	—	—	—	1	—	—	—	—	—
Before Ascension	608	50	196	5	50	29	1	2	—1	81	3	2	7	1	3
After Ascension	62	258	326	100	—	—	—	—	—	—	—	—	—	—	—
Total ..	670	308	522	105	50	30	1	2	1	81	3	2	7	1	3